Introduction

"The world is round and the place which may seem like the end may also be the only beginning."

Ivy Baker Priest

First and most importantly, let me tell you how happy I am that you have been so strong and obtained a freedom so often taken for granted! I am writing this with sadness in my heart that a need for this book even exists, but also with a determination for women to find their strength through the knowledge that there is a wonderful and fulfilling life waiting for you. It amazes me how people think of women that have been abused as weak. Abused women are the strongest people in the world. If you weren't strong, you wouldn't survive one day of it. I do believe, however, that the strength is being used in the wrong way the majority of the time. While enduring the abuse we use the strength to get through every day, walking on eggshells, wondering what will it be today; a beating, yelling, calling us every demeaning name in the book, throwing things at us, pulling our hair, choking us, even outright neglect for us as human beings. The best thing that we can do for ourselves is start using that strength to GET OUT!! We are afraid to leave, afraid of what might happen if we leave the abuser. We should be afraid of what will happen to us if we stay! If you are reading this, hopefully, you've already left. Whether you are in a family member's home, at a friend's, or in a shelter, this book is for you. I write this with a heartfelt wish for happiness and greatness in your life from this day forward!

I also want to thank all of my friends, who have been through abuse in some way or another who have inspired me to write this book and who have been there for me through the years. Abuse is all around us, we are not victims; we are SURVIVORS! Let us survive together and inspire each other to be positive in our thoughts and our actions and turn our lives around for the better. It's easier than you think...

Chapter 1: The Beginning

"Obstacles cannot crush me; every obstacle yields

to stern resolve."

Leonardo DaVinci

The first thing you need to get is a notebook and a pen. These items will prove to be indispensable for survival. The next things you need are a phone and a phone book. If you don't already have the courage to ask questions, take a deep breath, and let go of your fear, let go of negativity, let go of feeling that it can't be done. YOU CAN DO THIS! Start by making a list of the information that you need and where to get that information if you already know where to get it. If you don't know where to get it, I suggest dialing 211 or United Way. Be ready to write quickly and don't be afraid to ask the person on the other end of the line to repeat information if necessary. Also, don't be afraid to ask even if you think they might not have the answer; they may be able to direct you to someone who does, or if the next one doesn't either, they may know someone who does. One of the most beneficial lessons that I have learned over the last 5 years is "Ask questions, ask questions, and ask more questions!" Don't give up. Someone that you talk to either on the phone or in person has answers that you need. You may hesitate at first and think this is overwhelming, but trust me, the first time that you find one bit of information that you need, is like a lightning bolt of power. KNOWLEDGE IS POWER!!!! Don't ever forget that. This is why it is so important to talk to people. We cannot learn if we do not search for the answers. The answers don't just fall in our lap, unfortunately. It is a lot of work to survive, but every day brings more and more joy, strength, and respect from others, and most importantly, self-respect, and dignity. If you need some motivation, I suggest listening to empowering music, watch an empowering movie, write an inspiring message on your bathroom mirror, or find a mantra that when you say it, renews your strength. Do what you need to do to get motivated. You might even remember an instance or instances of abuse to be your driving force. The point is: find what works for you and use it. Also know that what works now, may need to be modified or changed altogether later on as you grow and find your unlimited inner strength that has been hidden away. Know that this amazing strength is and always has been there, and you are uncovering it day by day, step by step, breath by breath. Wow! Did you know that you had that strength inside you all this time? What a great epiphany to find it!

So you've called 211 and/or United Way, you've written down other phone numbers that you need. Some that you might need are:

1) Local utility companies (water, gas/electric)
   Some utility companies might have discounts for people with low-income.

2) Community Law Centers
   There are free to low-cost legal services available for you, but also keep in mind that if you can borrow money for an attorney, or have someone who will pay for an attorney for you, it can be worth it. Ask around to friends, family, neighbors, co-workers for referrals with attorneys, if you know someone who was pleased with a particular attorney and you can hire that person then that is less for you to worry about.

3) Local Police Department
   Call and report any abuse. This will help you now and in the future by having it documented as well as letting your abuser know that you will not be tolerating the abuse any longer and that if he does do something, he will be held accountable by the law. Some states have a law that will automatically give the case to the District Attorney's office so that it is out of your responsibility to keep the case going. Keep any and all cards from police officer's with the date of the call, what the call was about, their name, badge number, and phone number. Keep these in a safe place that you will have easy access to (I always kept mine in my purse, plus wrote down information on a calendar that I could carry with me when needed). I also highly recommend telling a friend about the abuse and being detailed about it. You need someone who can verify information. There is security in knowing someone who cares about you knows what you are going through and will be there for you when you need them.

4) Child Protective Services
   If you have children that are being abused, they need to be protected. Child Protective Services needs to be contacted to help you protect them.
   There is also an Abuse Hotline- 1-800-252-5400

5) Women's Protective Services

6) Rape Crisis Center

7) Suicide Crisis Line

One of the best lessons I ever learned in life is that EVERYTHING is temporary! That means that no matter how horrible life may seem to you right now that horrible feeling will NOT last forever! Work through it; do not throw your life away because of it. You are a very important person in the lives of many, and your life is a treasure. Do whatever you can to make your life better and get rid of that horrible feeling, but do NOT end your life. Call the professionals at the Suicide Crisis Line if you feel lost. They will help you immensely. The local number is in your phone book.

8) National Organization for Victim Assistance (NOVA)

1-800-TRY-NOVA (1-800-879-6682

9) National Coalition Against Domestic Violence

(202) 638-6388 or (303) 839-1852

10) District Attorney's Office

If you've had the abuser arrested and the DA's office now has the case. My biggest recommendation is to follow up often and do not give up. My personal case took over 2 years to finally go to court and get a conviction. It was worth the wait, worth the phone calls every month, worth the stress, worth every second of effort that I put into it. The prosecutor said that the only reason that he pled guilty was because I showed up to court. I had to travel 400 miles and miss 3 days of school to do it, but it was worth it. The police officer that makes the arrest will also be there, you are not alone. You can also be reimbursed for expenses that you incur due to the abuse (such as medical bills from the abuse, hotel and gasoline expenses for going to court, etc) by the Crime Victim's Compensation Division of the Attorney General's Office.

11) State Attorney General's Office

If you have children and will be receiving child support at some point, you will need to know the address and phone number of your local office. You can have them send you a pin number which you can use to check your child support payments online. The online update can give you information a day sooner than if you call the office, although sometimes you need to speak to someone at the office. If you have not received all of your child support, keep them aware of it by calling them. They can send letters, increase automatic deductions from the paychecks of the non-custodial parent, intercept tax refunds, military payments, workman's comp, unemployment insurance benefits, and more to make sure you receive what you and your children are entitled to receive.

12) Local Women's Shelter

If you do not have family or friends, or money for your own place, go to a shelter even if you just need it for a night or two. Don't be afraid to do this because of your children. You and your children are better off in a shelter with you than in an abusive home! They can get you what you need. They can even get you clothes for job interviews and can give you much needed information and connections.

13) Workforce Commission for your state

They can help you find a job that suits your abilities and needs as well as help you find childcare resources. The Workforce Commission also has lists of degree programs that the state will pay for your education to acquire!

14) Childcare Services

There are low-cost programs for daycare while you work and/or go to school to help you get on your feet financially. Some programs can even provide free daycare for your children if you are going to college for particular degrees.

15) Medicaid and Food Stamps

This is one of the best things that I did for my children (and myself too). Know that you are doing what you need to do to survive and keep the goal of making your life better and being able to get off of this in the future. These programs are there for a reason: to help you when you need it! Do not be ashamed or embarrassed to be on state assistance. You are absolutely doing what is best for you and your children to get on your feet and live on your own. If you are pregnant and low-income, you qualify for Medicaid too. Getting on Medicaid and maintaining it, takes effort on your part. There is an application and depending on your city, a long wait at the office, but again, so worth the effort! Remember too, that time is money. They may also be able to direct you to community health programs for women if you are not pregnant. Some cities have low-cost insurance programs through universities or just through the city or county itself. Keep asking until you find someone who knows the best answer for you. Taking care of yourself is a necessity whether you have children or not.

16) Colleges/Universities/Technical Schools

There is a lot of financial aid available and all you have to do is ask and keep asking. Apply for scholarships, internships, alternative loans, daycare programs. There is extra financial aid available for daycare, and most colleges have daycares on site for students with young children. Look into degree programs that you might be interested in. Get all of the information that you need from each school and print out the information! Apply at least 6 months before you plan on attending if at all possible.

5

Apply for FAFSA as soon after January 1st as you can. The earlier that you apply to FAFSA, the more financial aid you will receive. FAFSA determines your financial aid budget and rewards for everything except private scholarships. Know that if you get a scholarship that is not private and you've reached your limit on your budget, the school will subtract the amount of the scholarship from your loans. Private scholarships are great because they belong only to you and are not a part of your budget. Many universities have scholarships or programs for first generation college students as well. Research! Even if you start with a 2 year degree program, that may get you a job that ends up paying for you to get a Bachelor's degree or even a Master's degree. You would be amazed at what employers will offer to their employees to further their education. Remember what I said earlier, "KNOWLEDGE IS POWER!!" And I mean that with every ounce of my being. Apply to several different schools, even if they are in different cities from where you are now.

I realized that the worst thing anyone could tell me was "no" and that sometimes you have to hear several "no's" to get to a "yes". Also that "no" right now, may not mean "no" forever. That could turn into a yes later. Everyone told me that I would not be able to move to another city with my children after divorce. Guess what, my girls and I are now 400 miles away from their dad and I am going to Texas Tech University, and I am 40 years old. I didn't get here by thinking negatively and listening to those few people around me who don't know how determined I am. I took a chance, the opportunity was granted, and I took it without hesitation. And if you think you don't want to be poor going to school, remember that without a good education, you will more than likely not make decent money anyway. The time is going to pass whether you are in school or not so you may as well pass the time gaining immense knowledge and a degree that can further your position in society. Being in school is also a great way to network and make new friends. It's also very effective in helping you realize the power and knowledge that you already possess; in other words, it's a great self-esteem builder! The way I look at it is this: I would rather be extremely poor for a few years (7 and a half in my case) while I am in school, than poor for the rest of my life because I didn't go. Let me tell you again, "KNOWLEDGE IS POWER!!!!!" I hope I've made that point clear.....

17) Free Counseling Services

There are free counseling services available to those of us with no health insurance. Now these may be different counselors than who your children can see if they are on Medicaid. Go to counseling, even if you hate it and even if you can't bring yourself to do it except for those periods when you have low points. Sometimes they can refer you to a place that can help you with a particular issue that you might have, and they are certainly good people to vent to when you feel that your friends and family aren't quite enough for your needs. Free and low-cost counseling services can be found through United Way. By the way, did I mention that United Way will give you all of this information for free? That's why they are there. To help those who need it.

18) Credit Counseling Services

These will help you to get lower payments on debts. Also know that sometimes you can make a deal with a creditor and offer to pay them one lump sum of money that is substantially lower than what you owe and they will take it if they know that you might not ever be able to pay back the entire amount. I did this with a company and offered two thousand less than what I owed-they took it! Also, as long as you make an effort in paying a bill, even if it is $1.00 per month, they can't do anything about it--------you are making an effort. Also keep in mind that many and most creditors will work with you as long as you contact them and keep them up to date on your situation. People end up in trouble when they hide from their creditors due to inability to pay. Always be up front with them and they are usually accommodating. Granted, you might end up with higher interest rates, but that is better than a lawsuit against you for non-payment. Some creditors are even willing to lower your interest rate for you and all you have to do is ask them when you tell them your situation.

19) Apartment Guides and Apartment Locators

I personally like the apartment locators. These people will help you find exactly what you need in your price range. They are free to you as they get paid by the place that you rent from. They do all the work for you! How great is that? That's another thing you don't have to have to worry about. The Apartment Guides are books that tell you all of the apartments in your area, their locations, amenities, and restrictions.

20) Religious Organizations/Churches

These can help you not only with your religious and spiritual needs, but be a source of hope, compassion, hugs, and a refuge from your stress. Many churches, especially Catholic Charities, have programs for low-income people to get food, clothing, school supplies, and even rental and/or utility assistance. Keep in mind that some of these may only be used one time a year, but you can apply every year that you need help and it just takes a little bit of extra time that will help you out tremendously.

21) Section 8 Housing

Depending on where you live, there might be a long wait list. GET ON IT even if you think you may not need it by the time it is offered to you. It is always better to be safe than sorry. Know also that in larger cities, there may be more than one Section 8 program. There may be a city and a county program. Find which one is right for you depending on your situation.

22) Habitat For Humanity

I go to school with a single mom of 4 children who just moved into her 3 bedroom home that she helped build with Habitat for Humanity. Apparently, like everything else, it is a lot of paperwork, and takes effort, but its rewards are immeasurable if you qualify. Remember, it never hurts to ask or to try. I've found that my biggest regrets are not the things I've done, but the things I didn't do. Don't be afraid to ask. If they say you don't qualify, then at least you tried, right?

23) If you have pets, find out about low-cost to free animal care services such as vaccinations and spay and neutering services. Some cities have a program called SNAP (Spay Neuter Assistance Program). Many times, there are low-cost clinics at feed stores as well. Take advantage of this for your pets, as they deserve to be healthy too. It is worth your effort to have a healthy pet. Illnesses such as parvovirus are so easy to prevent with a simple vaccination but cost a lot of money to treat; or worse, you end up without your beloved companion who is better than a human and will always love you unconditionally.

24) Ask wherever you need if they have discounts for low-income families and/or students if that is your situation. The places that will offer discounts for services might surprise you.

25) Free Income Tax Services

You can call the IRS for the name and number of the program in your area.

26) Free or low-cost Prescriptions

Ask your physician's office for programs to get needed prescriptions at low or no cost. Also, if you are attending college, go to the health center at your college. Many times you can get prescriptions from their office to be filled at a discounted rate through a pharmacy they have a contract with.

27) Free and reduced lunch program

Public schools have free or reduced price meals for children who are on Medicaid.

28) Pre-K programs through Public Schools

Children of families on Medicaid or food stamps can go to Pre-k at public schools at age 4 in some communities. Check with your school district for information on what they have to offer.

Chapter 2: Filing & Paperwork

"Our greatest glory is not in never failing,

but in rising up every time we fall."

Ralph Waldo Emerson

I hope that list helps you out. Now some of those you may not need, or you may need something that is not there, but that should get you going pretty well. Remember to ask United Way or call 211 if there is something else you need taken care of; they should be able to send you in the right direction.

Now that you've got your list going, the phone numbers are in your phone book either in the blue pages or under city, county, or state government phone number listings. Please be patient and know that some of these places are extremely busy and you may need to hold awhile. Please do not give up, your time and effort will be rewarded to you as these places will help you gain more freedom and ease your load.

Now you need to start some files for the paperwork from these different agencies and offices. Make extra copies of leases, utility bills, medical bills, taxes, paycheck stubs, bank accounts, etc. as you will need these for more than one of these offices for different applications you fill out. You will also need your children's birth certificates if you have kids, as well as social security cards for anyone that is on the application. Be prepared every six months to reapply for food stamps and Medicaid. Be diligent about filling these out on time as being without them for even a week or two can prove detrimental. Remember, this is all to help you get on your own financially and will ease your stress immensely. The more organized you are, the better off you will be and it makes everything so much easier! Keep the papers all together in a place you can access easily and quickly. A small file box works great. I also like to use colored folders that catch my eye for the papers that I use the most often.

I also make a list of papers that I am going to need for each application so that I can check them off before going to the office. Then I make sure that I have all of the copies that I need for that appointment together before I ever leave the house. Also know that some places will consider you a no-show and will cancel your appointment if you are more than 5 to 10 minutes late. Be very mindful of being on time so that you are not put in a difficult situation financially because of a few minutes of time. Remember, time is money. What you put in with your effort, you get back in saving money and stress.

A journal or an extra notebook is also going to be needed if you have not had one going already to log any and all abuse or arguments with your ex regarding the children (or arguing with or abusing you if you don't have children). Be sure and log everything, even if it doesn't seem like a big deal, it might end up being essential later. Be sure and put the date and time and great details of any incidences, as well as phone calls. Log harassment that you receive via phone calls, showing up unannounced, cussing at you, anything that you might need documentation of. Be sure and call the police and make reports if this is ongoing. It may take a month or so of journaling harassment to be able to make a police report. Then make the report by going to the police station with your log dates, times, and what happened and you've got it done. Let the police handle it from there. Now this is difficult sometimes, but again, something you need to do. Sometimes all it takes is telling your ex that you filed a police report and they will stop. But I would not tell them that without having actually filed one as you wouldn't want them to find out you lied to them. That's another thing, if you feel you can't be honest, don't say anything. Let them be the one to slip up. Watch what you do. Be responsible and mindful for all of your actions. If you need to vent and be angry, hopefully, you have a good friend that will let you release your frustrations by screaming about it to them, not screaming at your ex. Abusers tend to be very calm around everyone else trying to convince everyone around that you are the one that is unstable because you get mad and yell. Do your best to be calm, but very firm in what you say. If you have to walk away or hang up the phone, that is better than saying something that can be used against you later. Slow deep breaths and a visual thought is a good way to redirect your attention and let your mood lighten. One of my favorite quotes is "Power means never having to respond". I have kept this quote in a place I can see it often for several years. It's amazing how many times it's saved me from saying something I shouldn't!

In some states, it is legal to tape record someone without telling them as long as the person tape recording is a part of the conversation. Please check with your local police department or your attorney to find out about this. If it is legal, this could really save you….it might literally save your life or your children's lives. I recommend the small handheld tape recorders. In fact, now the recorders are usually digital and usually cost about $30. I know it's a lot, but if it saves your life, then it is priceless. Be sure and have dates and times on the recording so that you can prove when the conversation took place.

Chapter 3: Taking Care of You

"Dare to live the life you have dreamed for yourself.

Go forward and make your dreams come true."

Ralph Waldo Emerson

O.K. Now it's time for a break. I hope you find this refreshing after the previous heavy talk. You know how when you're on a plane and they tell you that if the air pressure drops and the oxygen masks come down, that you need to breathe from it first BEFORE children or the elderly? They say this because if you don't take care of yourself, you will not be well enough to take care of anyone else. Well, the same thing applies in life in any given situation. If we are falling apart at the seams, are angry, stressed, or feeling uncared for, how can we be good friends, mothers, daughters, sisters, employees? The answer is, we can't. The best thing we can do for ourselves and those around us is to take care of ourselves FIRST. This is not selfish. Remember, everyone is better off if we feel cared for. The only person that we can ever really depend on to take care of us is ourselves. Now, this takes some getting used to if you've been used to putting everyone else first your entire life. You will find that it gets easier and that it works very well. I personally like some very intense exercise as it is great at getting out frustration, anger, and best of all releases endorphins that last ALL DAY! My girls tell me, "Mommy, you seem pretty stressed, I think you'd better get to the gym today." They say that, because they know firsthand what works and that if I'm happy, then they will benefit immensely. Exercise also helps you sleep better, look better, and feel better about yourself inside and out. Reading a book is a good break, watching a movie, taking a bath after the kids go to sleep, dancing around the house, cooking, or even cleaning while listening to some feel-good music. Find out what works best for you and your personality.

My friends and I depend on each other a lot, too. I have several friends in similar situations and we talk on the phone almost daily, even if it is just to say "Hi". Having someone in your life that truly understands what you are going through is extremely helpful. I try to keep my issues regarding my ex to those particular friends, just because they can relate. There are a lot of people that can't understand just because of their situation. Please don't let this frustrate you; just accept it and know that there are others around you that do know exactly how you feel and who will always be there for you. A good thing to do is just vent, let them vent if they need to, and then start joking around. Get it out and be done with it for that day. If you keep a positive attitude the majority of the time, then positive things will happen for you the majority of the time! My friends and I are good about joking about some otherwise serious situations. It's either laugh or cry; and frankly, I'd rather laugh, it's a lot more fun! Remember that sometimes something that seems bad right now can be a huge blessing down the road. This is tough to remember sometimes and it's wonderful to have a good friend to remind you of that when you need it. Another one of the great things I've learned in life is that everything is impermanent. Remind yourself of this next time you are feeling overwhelmed. It will pass, and happiness is just around the corner if you decide you want to find it.

Another thing I recommend is signing up for inspirational email messages from various websites that you may find. If you do not have a computer at home, you can use a computer at a public library for free. I get messages daily that start my day off with a good attitude and this is a big blessing in my life. Attitude is everything. Our minds are very powerful, and with the right attitude, we can accomplish anything we put our minds to!

Chapter 4: Breaking the Cycle

"Things don't go wrong and break your heart so you can become bitter and give up. They happen to break you down and build you up so you can be all that you were intended to be."

-- Charles "Tremendous" Jones

In recovering from abuse, and finding our strength, our personalities change tremendously. This is a difficult thing for people who have been in our lives for a long time to adjust to. They are used to treating us a certain way (usually walking all over us and controlling us). This is difficult for them, because they didn't change, we did. They are resistant to our new-found "Self". They are used to us doing whatever they tell us to do, even if it is something small and that may seem insignificant in their point of view. Our relationships with others are fragile and must be nourished, but in order to be strong, we need to be firm with those we love in setting our boundaries of control. It is like a dance. If someone is always used to being the lead, it is difficult for them to start being the follower and if you are used to following what everyone tells you to do, it is difficult to be the leader. You need to start to take the lead. It is YOUR life. I have been criticized for being too harsh with things I've said to those whom I love more than anything in this world. But to be honest, I had to be harsh to get them to realize that I meant business. I was tired of being controlled. There's a fine line sometimes between help and control, and we must define it clearly and not allow it to be crossed. That being said, with what we've been through, sometimes when people try to help us, it feels as if they are trying to control us and we become resistant to their help. This is not easy. We need to step back and take some deep breaths and really see it for what it IS, not what it feels like to us at the moment. If people are used to crossing that line of control (usually because they don't know it exists), it is not easy for them not to cross it. Like training a dog, we must be firm over and over again, and eventually, they will learn not to cross that line with us. This also helps them to have more respect for us. Would you respect someone who let you control them all of the time? The answer is no. We respect those who stand up for themselves and what they need and do what is best for them. We must respect ourselves enough to stand our ground and make that line

15

visible and bold, so that those who were used to running right over it will stop in their tracks before they reach it. They will have respect enough for us to know that we can and will control our own lives.

The best word I ever learned to say was "NO". What amazing power there is in that very little word. The first time that I said no to someone, was one of the best moments in my life and I remember it very clearly. It was such a powerful moment and gave me such elation, that I called my family and friends immediately to tell them what I had said and how wonderful I felt doing that. Saying no was not mean, it was just me having control of my life for the first time. Don't say yes to anything that you really don't want to do. Be honest with yourself and others. Being true to ourselves is a great gift to us and those around us. Learn to say no and don't feel guilty because you didn't let someone walk all over you. Trust me, they will not like your new-found freedom, and it may even take them years to get used to it, but they will eventually learn and respect you for it. In order for this to work though, you must be consistent. If you are not consistent, they will not learn. The more you stand up for yourself, the easier it gets. Please be kind in your strength and firmness as much as you possibly can. Integrity is a virtue and a great virtue to possess. Also remember that great quote, "Power means never having to respond." Sometimes, the best thing you can do is not say anything at all. My suggestion is that if you are in a heated argument with someone who unknowingly is trying to control you that you tell them very firmly that you will not discuss it at the moment, and that you both need to calm down and let the emotions cool off before talking about it again. Apologize for getting angry, but don't be sorry for standing up for yourself. Remember, it's learning to dance with this person differently than either of you ever have before; it is not easy at times, and sometimes, we just need a time-out to regroup. It's perfectly ok and everyone involved will benefit.

Remember that you are a wonderful and deserving human being. Do not settle on having people in your life who will not help you make your life better if those people are not essential in your life (ie; if they are not family). Choose to have healthy relationships and nothing less. If you have friends in your life that are always bringing you down, it is time to know that those relationships are not benefiting you and they need to be put on the back burner or deleted altogether. Keeping people in your life that will fully support you in your goal to make your life better is the key to your success. We are human and we all need each other, but we don't need people in our lives who do not further our progress. Remember, you are a wonderful, deserving, and strong woman. You are amazing!!

Chapter 5: Words from the Wise

"Keep your face in the sunshine and you can never see the shadow."
-- Helen Keller

I wanted to end this short book with some of my favorite quotes that I hope will inspire you as they have inspired me. You've been through a lot. Do not dwell on that, but dwell instead on making your life better every day!

"Forgiveness is letting go of the anger, that's all. It doesn't mean we excuse, or forget, or condone the behavior that caused the anger- whether the anger is directed at ourselves, or others, or both."

"Power means never having to respond"

"We must be willing to get rid of the life we've planned so as to have the life that is waiting for us." *--Joseph Campbell, writer*

"It isn't the greatest pleasures that count the most; it's making a great deal out of the little ones." *---Jean Webster*

"I never lose sight of the fact that just being is fun."

---Katherine Hepburn

"You cannot discover new oceans unless you have the courage to lose sight of the shore."

"Pain is inevitable, suffering is not."

----Bhante Henepola Gunaratana

"One's first step in wisdom is to question everything- and one's last is to come to terms with everything."

---Georg Christoph Lichtenberg (1742-1799)

"Like taking a morning shower, make the planting of positive thoughts a daily practice." -- Neil Eskelin

Not knowing when the dawn will come I open every door.

---Emily Dickinson (1830–1886)

"The only limitation in your life is the limitation of your own thinking." -- James A. Ray

"Continuous effort - not strength or intelligence - is the key to unlocking our potential."   --- Sir Winston Churchill

"It is one of the most beautiful compensations in life that no man can sincerely try to help another without helping himself."

---Ralph Waldo Emerson (1803-1882)

"The ability to adapt is everything!" ---Denis Waitley

"The secret of health for both mind and body is not to mourn for the past, worry about the future, or anticipate troubles, but to live in the present moment wisely and earnestly." ----Buddha

"Our greatest glory is not in never failing, but in rising up every time we fall." ---Ralph Waldo Emerson

Only those who see the invisible can do the impossible.

"Courage is the price that Love extracts for granting peace."

---Amelia Earhart

"We cannot become what we need to be by remaining what we are." ----Max Dupree

"Most of us are about as happy as we make our minds up to be."

---Abraham Lincoln

"Life is just a chance to grow a soul." ---A. Powel Davies

"Dare to live the life you have dreamed for yourself. Go forward and make your dreams come true." ---Ralph Waldo Emerson

"There's nothing better than a good friend, except a good friend with CHOCOLATE." ---Linda Grayson, The Pickwick Papers

"Spend each moment perfecting the next, not correcting the last."

---Scott Michael Durski

"To accomplish great things, we must dream as well as act."

---Anatole France

"Courage is not the absence of fear, but rather the knowledge that something else is more important than fear." -The Princess Diary

"What lies behind us and what lies before us are tiny matters compared to what lies within us." ---Ralph Waldo Emerson

"Peace is a journey, not a destination!"

"Good, better, best. Never let it rest. Until your good is better and your better is best." ---Tim Duncan, San Antonio Spurs

"When I dare to be powerful, to use my strength in the service of my vision, then it becomes less and less important whether I am afraid."

----Audre Lorde

"Whatever you can do or dream you can, begin it. Boldness has a genius, power, and magic in it." ---Johann Wolfgang Von Goethe

"Victory comes, at times, just when one no longer expects it."

---Martin Buber (1878-1965)

"Nothing great was ever achieved without enthusiasm."

---Ralph Waldo Emerson

"Nothing gives a person so much advantage over another as to remain cool and unruffled under all circumstances."

---Thomas Jefferson

"Challenge everything you do. Expand your thinking. Refocus your efforts. Rededicate yourself to your future." ---Patricia Fripp

"Mastery is not something that strikes in an instant, like a thunderbolt, but a gathering of power that moves steadily through time, like the weather." ---John Champlin Gardner, Jr.

"Some people, no matter how old they get, never lose their beauty—they merely move it from their faces into their hearts."

---Martin Buxbaum (1912-1991)

"You can't think your way into acting positively, but you can act your way into thinking positively." ---Nido Qubein

"Imitate until you emulate. Match and surpass those who launched you. It's the highest form of thankfulness." ---Mark Victor Hansen

"We don't remain good if we don't always strive to be better."

---Gottfried Ketter (1819-1890)

"Goodness is the only investment that never fails."

---Henry David Thoreau (1817-1862)

Pain is nothing compared to what it feels like to give in.

Dream. Focus. Live. Love.

"To one who has faith, no explanation is necessary. To one without faith, no explanation is possible." –Thomas Aquinas (c.1224-1274)

"In actual life, every great enterprise begins with and takes its first forward step in faith." ---Friedrich von Schlegal (1772-1829)

"Patience makes lighter what sorrow may not heal." –Horace

"Conquer anger with lack of anger; bad, with good; stinginess, with generosity; a liar, with truth."

---Dhammapada 17, translated by Thanissaro Bhikku

"We are what we repeatedly do. Excellence, therefore, is not an act, but a habit." ---Aristotle

"To get what we've never had, we must do what we've never done."

---Anonymous

"Courage is fear holding on a minute longer."

---General George S. Patton

American Soldier and General (1885-1945)

"Many of life's failures are men who did not realize how close they were to success when they gave up."

---Thomas Edison

American Inventor (1847-1931)

Triumph often is nearest when defeat seems inescapable."

---B.C. Forbes (1880-1954)

"In the confrontation between the stream and the rock, the stream always wins...not by strength, but by perseverance."

---H. Jackson Brown

"Whether you think you can, or think you can't...you're right."

---Henry Ford

"Perseverance is not a long race: it is many short races, one after another." ---Walter Elliot

"The life that conquers is the life that moves with a steady resolution and persistence toward a predetermined goal. Those who succeed are those who have thoroughly learned the immense importance of plan in life, and the tragic brevity of time." --- W.J. Davison

"Nobody can go back and start a new beginning, but anyone can start today and make a new ending." -- Maria Robinson

"I've learned that no matter what happens, or how bad it seems today, life does go on, and it will be better tomorrow." -- Maya Angelou

"It is funny about life; if you refuse to accept anything but the very best you will very often get it." -- W. Somerset Maugham

"Just to be is a blessing, just to live is holy."

---Abraham Joshua Heschel (1907-1972)

Philosopher and theologian

And last, but certainly not least:

"Never, Never, Never Give Up."

---Winston Churchill